YPS

Please return / renew by date shown.
You can renew it at:
norlink.norfolk.gov.uk
or by telephone: 0344 800 8006
Please have your library card & PIN ready

PLAYGROUP COLLECTION

space.

IN SPACE

Sun

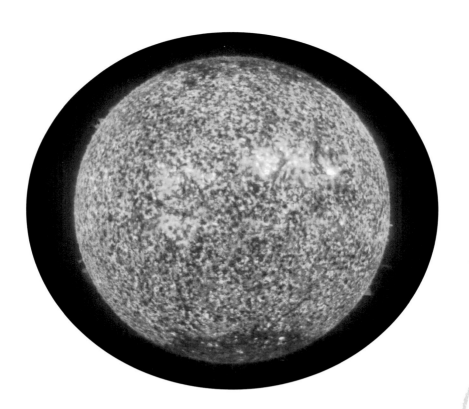

Chris Oxlade

WAYLAND

Explore the world with **Popcorn** - your complete first non-fiction library.

Look out for more titles in the **Popcorn** range. All books have the same format of simple text and striking images. Text is carefully matched to the pictures to help readers to identify and understand key vocabulary.
www.waylandbooks.co.uk/popcorn

First published in 2009 by Wayland
Copyright Wayland 2009

Wayland
Hachette Children's Books
338 Euston Road
London NW1 3BH

Wayland Australia
Level 17/207 Kent Street
Sydney NSW 2000

Editor: Julia Adams
Designer: Robert Walster
Picture researcher: Julia Adams

British Library Cataloguing in Publication Data
Oxlade, Chris.
    Sun. -- (Popcorn. In space)
    1. Sun--Juvenile literature.
    I. Title II. Series
    523.7-dc22
ISBN 978 0 7502 5776 3

Printed and bound in China

Wayland is a division of Hachette Children's Books,
an Hachette UK Company

www.hachette.co.uk

Acknowledgements:
Alamy: NASA images 10, imagebroker 11,
Corbis Super RF 13, Alex Segre 18, Will
Stanton 19, Terrance Klassen 21;
iStockphoto: Andreas Weber 20; Science
Photo Library: Detlev van Ravenswaay 4/5,
Mehau Kulyk 9, John Foster 17,
SOHO/ESA/NASA 8, Roger Harris 7, John
Bova 16; Shutterstock: Nataliya Peregudova
2, 15, silver-john 12, emphimy 14; SOHO
(ESA & NASA): OFC; Andy Crawford: 22, 23;

☀ Contents

The solar system 4

Sun and Earth 6

Stars 8

Day-time 10

Sunshine 12

Night-time 14

Moonlight 16

The Sun and life 18

Solar energy 20

Day and night 22

Glossary 24

Index 24

 The solar system

Earth is where we live. It is a planet.
It belongs to a group of eight planets.
All these planets get light and heat
from the Sun.

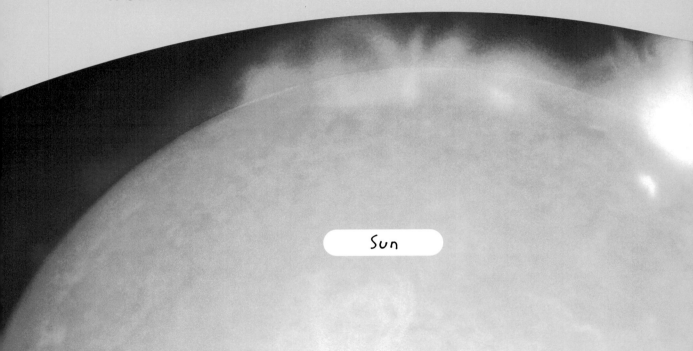

Sun

The eight planets travel around
the Sun in giant circles called orbits.
The Sun and the planets are called
the solar system.

Uranus

Neptune

Mars

Venus

Saturn

Jupiter

Earth

Mercury

 Sun and Earth

The Sun is a giant ball of glowing gas. It shines rays of heat and light that travel through space. They light up all the planets in the solar system.

The Sun is 70 times wider than the Earth.

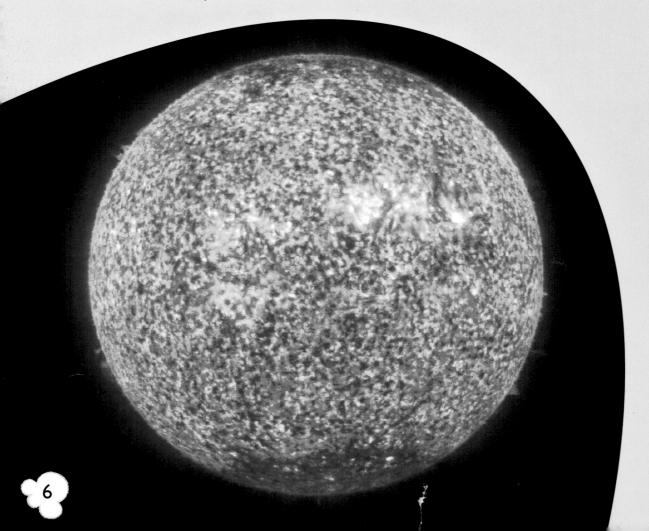

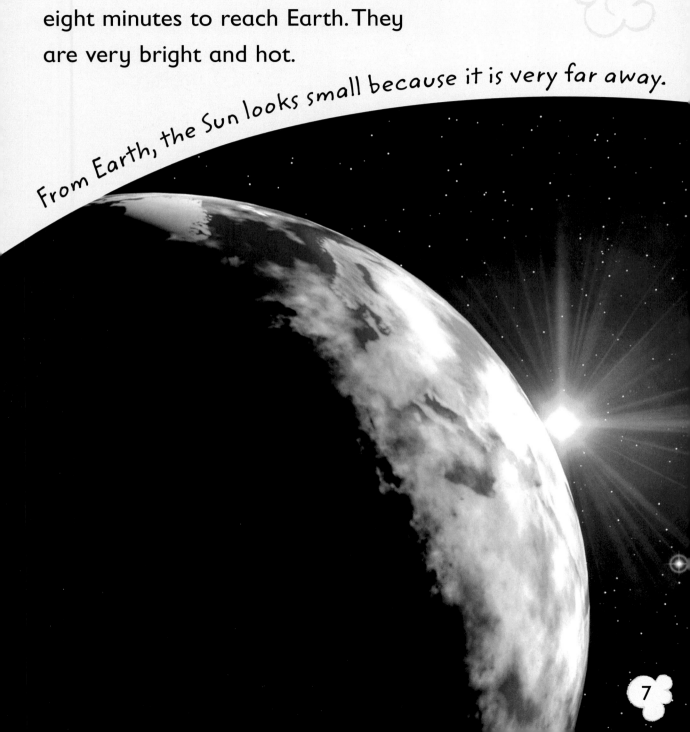

The rays of the Sun take more than
eight minutes to reach Earth. They
are very bright and hot.

From Earth, the Sun looks small because it is very far away.

 # Stars

The Sun is a star. The tiny specks
of light in the night sky are stars,
too. A star is an object in space
that gives off light and heat.

The surface of the Sun is hotter than
anything on Earth.

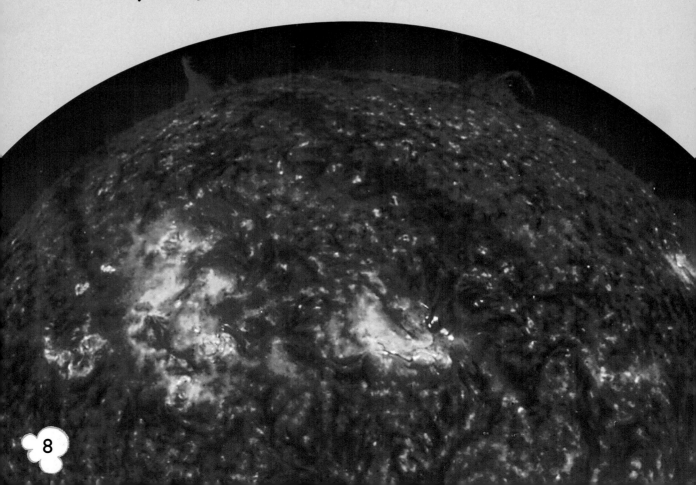

The Sun is a medium-sized star.
Some stars are larger than the
Sun and some are smaller.

You can see many
stars on a clear
night. They are
all further
away than
the Sun.

Day-time

The Earth spins round once every day.
It is day-time when the place where
you live faces the Sun.

The Sun
only ever
shines on
one side of
the Earth.

Day-time begins when the Sun
rises into the sky.

The Sun rises at a different time each day.

Can you
find out what
time the Sun
rises?

☀ Sunshine

When the Sun shines on our part of the Earth, it gives us light and warmth.

Plants need sunshine to grow.

Sunshine is very bright, so we need
to be careful. Sunscreen protects
our skin from the heat of the Sun.

Without sunscreen our skin can get burnt.

☀ Night-time

It is night-time when the place where
you live faces away from the Sun. Then it
is day-time on the other side of the Earth.

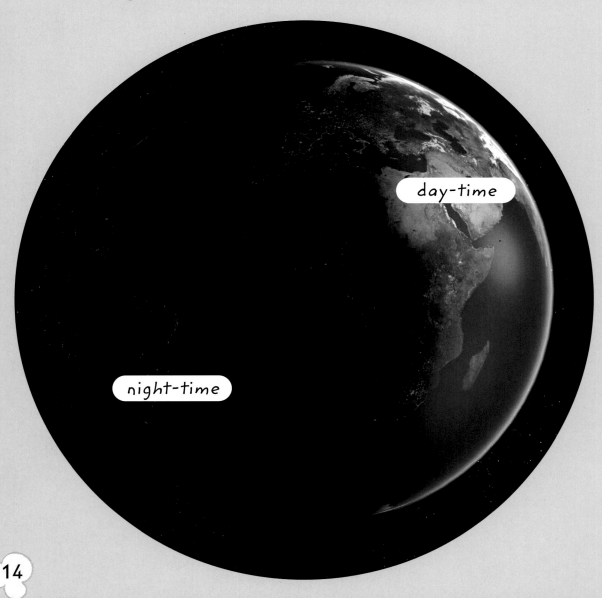

day-time

night-time

At the end of day-time the Sun
goes down in the sky.

Night-time begins at sunset.

The part
of the day
when the Sun
sets is called
dusk.

15

 # Moonlight

On a clear night, you can see the Moon in the sky. The Moon does not make its own light. It is lit up by the Sun.

The Sun only lights up one side of the Moon.

The Moon reflects the light from the Sun to Earth. This is called moonlight.

We only see the part of the Moon that is lit up by the Sun.

☀ The Sun and life

Without sunshine the Earth would be a very cold and dark place. There would be no day-light or moonlight.

Heat from the Sun makes the Earth warm.

On other planets in the solar system it is too hot or cold for things to live.

Without the Sun we would not have any food to eat. Plants and animals could not live here.

Without sunshine there would be no fruit or vegetables.

☀ Solar energy

The Sun can give us energy. We use energy to make cars move, to work machines, to cook and to keep warm.

These solar panels use the sunshine to heat water.

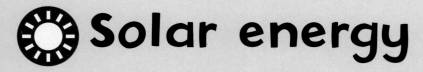

We can make electricity from the sunlight. We use solar panels to power some watches, street lamps, calculators and even cars.

This car is powered by the Sun's energy.

Day and night

See how sunshine gives us day and night.

You will need:
• a tennis ball (or a ball the same size as a tennis ball)
• a pen • string
• sticky tape
• a torch

1. Use a ruler to measure 30 cm of string.

2. Cut the string. Use sticky tape to attach the string to the ball.

3. With a pen, mark a dot on the ball. This represents where you live.

4. In a darkened room, hold the string so that the ball hangs in the air.

5. Ask a friend to shine a torch at the ball from about two metres away. The torch represents the Sun. One side of the ball will be lit up.

6 Spin the ball slowly. Can you see the dot having day-time then night-time?

23

Glossary

ray light or heat that travels in straight lines

reflects when light bounces off something

solar panel a panel that collects heat from the Sun or changes sunlight into electricity

star an object in space that gives off light and heat

sunset when the Sun disappears behind the land

Index

Earth 4, 5, 6, 7, 8, 10, 12, 18

day-time 10, 11, 14, 15

energy 20, 21

Moon 16, 17
moonlight 16, 17, 18
morning 11

night-time 14, 15, 16, 17

orbit 5

planet 4, 5, 6, 18
plant 12, 19

sky 8, 9, 11, 15, 16
solar panels 20
solar system 4, 5, 18
star 8, 9
Sun 4, 5, 6, 7, 8, 9, 10, 11, 12,
    13, 14, 15, 16, 17, 18, 19,
    20, 21
sunrise 11
sunset 15
sunshine 10, 12, 13